How to:

Release Your Savage

"Motivation for Teens and Young Adults"

By Author: Rico Piddington

"DUDE! That was SAVAGE!" he said. I love when someone shows themself to be successful in something others said couldn't be done. I feel like it shows the planet that we aren't just a bunch of mammals looking for validation in the opinions of our peers. It also shows others what they are capable of. Think about it, it was thought to be impossible to run a mile in under 4 minutes... until someone actually did it! Savage? I think so.

In a world where people are constantly watched and appraised, it SEEMS that the only true comfort lies is the validation of our peers. However, what if I told you that as we evolve, so do the tools and strategies used by life to equalize its test and keep life hard enough to separate those who are *destined for greatness* and those who are *doomed to seek acceptance*. What if I told you it was the Savage inside of us all?

Let this book be a reinforcement for you or a new catalyst to ignite your potential. Just let it remind you of who you really are and that its perfectly alright to be a complete and utter Savage! Let me just take a moment and spit about what this book will examine, give, and teach you so that you can release your potential to the fullest.

Spitters Notes

I've come to learn some of life hardest lessons through the pain and suffering of failure after repeated failure. I feel very strongly on a great many topics and wish to share everything I have learned through both my failures and those I hold to be the Savages of the world.

The points I will touch on will probably range from literally one side of the spectrum where lifestyles and major life choices are made, to the other side of the spectrum where religion and family reside. I will try to share everything while motivating you to take that chance and your the inner savage out.

I will literally share some of the very same principles that have influenced the greatest minds, entrepreneurs, and millionaires alive (and in history). I will help you unlock the savage living inside you that's not afraid to change the game and make the hard choices you must make to succeed.

Now, I have a fine lust for the quant things in life. Things like fast foods, television, and video games. After all, are these not the bedrock, the bread and butter, are these not the solid foundations of the greats (lol!)? I certainly used to think so. Until I started watching and actually studying the greats.

What I found was extremely profound. It wasn't the love of any kind of luxuries that had the greats plotting their crusades long before they were ever even greats. It was actually something completely different. The something I will share with you in chapter 1 of this book.

Chapter: 1
"What is a Savage?"

Many of you picked this book up because you want to know if you are already a savage. To the disappointment of many of you reading this right now, you will learn that you are not yet a savage. You will also learn that everything you need to become a savage is already inside you. The best part is, it doesn't take much to unlock it either, to take control of your life and make it worth something greater than it is right now. In fact, you are one HUGE step closer just by picking up this book. This may only be the first book you read, but you will see as you read more and more books, that you are getting ever closer to your goal and a truly savage game on the court of life.

Let's start your training off by learning a few things. I consider the next five chapters you will read, to be a tiny insight into the direction you should seek out and follow to succeed in life.

In this chapter we are going to cover the 5 MAJOR qualities that make you a proud *savage of success*. These five qualities undeniably make a savage what they are. This is because every legend that lives today, acquired that status directly due to their allocation and use of these qualities. Because these qualities hold a Savage up, we will call them pillars.

These are the single most valuable attributes anyone could ever hope to add to their arsenal while staying disciplined enough to live full lives they can enjoy. Personally, I call these the mega pillars of power. Remember, a Savage is not a Savage without a valuable differentiator. Safe to say, these five mega pillars of pure power are what make a Savage.

PILLAR 1: DRIVE

I want you to imagine, if you can, a huge pillar made of gold, dwarfing tall over all 4 other pillars. It's glistening with a yellow glow of power all around it. This gigantic monstrosity of architecture is the first pillar and by far the biggest pillar. The pillar is only a metaphor, but a massive symbol for how much of your success relies on the first pillar.

This first mega pillar is *Drive*. Drive is the fuel that burns and powers the operation of successful habits. For this reason, a Savage must keep their drive fresh and powerful enough to keep the going strong. Every Savage relies heavily on this pillar because like any engine, its operation is most reliant upon its source of fuel.

Drive can be compared to motivation. This is because of how it works. Motivation needs refreshing and recharging <u>every single day</u>. When a Savage misses a day and doesn't motivate themselves, they are sure to feel the difference in performance and definitely in attitude. Here is where their level of confidence will fall short. And let's face it, no one has ever seen a savage that doesn't have confidence. Therefore, drive is an indispensable quality of a savage.

Now, there are special methods a Savage can use to ensure they stay motivated and Driven every day. Using these methods can do two things for them and you. 1) It gives them the fullness they seek each day and 2) It's a unique strategy that helps keep the momentum needed for all high performers. Let's dive into the method Savages use for keeping their Drive unmatched by ordinary people; those who have no Drive.

SAVAGE KEY: Motivation

I once heard it said that motivation is like showering. It took me a while to realize the gravity of how right that individual was. If you're a hard worker, putting your all into your job, you can't expect one shower at the beginning of the week, to keep you clean and fresh throughout the entire week. Likewise, a serious Savage knows that motivating once a week isn't going to cut it.

But how do you keep yourself motivated all week? If you're like every other human alive, then you can't expect yourself not to get bored of using the same method day in and day out. So, let's talk about the various methods you can use every day of your life to excel and dominate the court of life.

Morning Motivation is the first and most yielding, or giving, of all other types of motivation. If you pay attention, you can find it on the schedule of every highly successful Savage. Remember, the strongest Savages alive, know and have shared, that a strong foundation rooted in the morning, paves the road for a fierce advantage for anyone's day.

Motivational videos are just unwanted teaching to most, but to a real Savage, they are the most important tool they can incorporate into their daily routines. There are many different platforms you can use including social platforms and/or media platforms that offer TONS of great content for motivating and inspiring Savages early in the morning.

Media has become one of the world's greatest motivators. You can search sites like YouTube to find a new video for every day, for decades. And the diversity is absolutely outstanding. Taking a quick 5 minutes out of your morning routine to get yourself pumped for the day has NEVER been so easy OR important. Don't lose out on this highly underrated secret of the greats.

We will soon learn more about how videos effect our learning, but for now let's just talk about the types of motivation a Savage looks for early in the morning; what helps them start their day off right. Motivating early helps thrust them forward into the day so they can get those extreme results.

Videos are by far the best way to self-motivate for some, but for others, there may be a better way. Reading a chapter out of a great self-improvement book (like this one) could be the case for you. This method is one for those that don't live alone or don't have much space to themselves (I.e., you have a lot of siblings). The ones with little privacy or that may share a room at home or college. Maybe this is the preferred method of motivation for someone living way out in the middle of nowhere, on an island, with only their soccer ball for a friend. Either way, you can't go wrong here either.

Don't be afraid to search out those books that do it for you. The diversity in the literary world is just as diverse as the world of motivational videos. There are books on finance, health, mental strength, focus, goals, memory, leadership, and so many more, including motivation and inspiration!

Still, there are many more ways to motivate yourself early in the morning. Some have found that a quick 15-minute exercise routine to some high-tempo music does the trick for them. Even scientists have proven that exercise can boost mental focus, confidence, and energy levels throughout your entire day.

Many people wouldn't dream of getting out of their cozy bed to exercise, but that's why they will never be Savages, just big soft marshmallows. Your job is to make them think you're out of your mind. To make them think there is no way they can do what you do. Show them what a real Savage is and what a real Savage does.

Now, remember, if you don't have the time in the morning, wakeup earlier and make the time. Savages didn't get the name by going with the flow. They didn't become what they are by only grinding when they had time, no. They made time where there wasn't any. A true Savage of success creates his/her own flow and then grinds the living hell out of it! They **develop the habits** that **develop them**.

Recreational Motivation is the second major way a Savage finds his motivation. This is the motivation they find from the choices they've made and followed through on; joining the gym, reading a new book, taking an educational class or seminar, learning something new, or just adding a new hobby that improves the quality of their life.

Listen to me. Recreational motivation may not be as important as the routine you build your day with, but it can be just as effective. There are tips to using recreational motivation that Savages have learned and use each and every single day.

The first is follow through. **A true Savage never quits**. The real Savage knows that success only comes from making up their mind, acting on that decision, and seeing it through all the way, no matter comes up. They always see the mission through. They **Decide, Commit, and Succeed**.

Environmental Motivation is the final major type of motivation a Savage can find is indispensable. Environmental motivation is the posters, sticky notes, and pictures you hang around where you can see them. Environmental motivation comes from friends YOU CHOOSE to have around you, the places YOU CHOOSE to hangout, and the foods YOU CHOOSE to eat.

Environmental motivation is **the environment you create to live in and expose yourself to**. It's the atmospheres you stay in, on the daily bases. A REAL Savage creates the perfect environment for success. If the perfect environment for them doesn't exist, they develop it and manage it. Savages do not let outsiders interrupt their plans for success or their dreams. No one stops them from completing their missions or reaching their goals.

Now, the true Savages have found the best possible ways to develop their environments. A real Savage is all about the right environment.

They do not associate themselves with anyone that could side-track them from their goals (the bad influencers). They don't waste time or money like the masses do, entertaining their peers with their knowledge of memes or favorite TikTok videos.

The hardest Savages thin the heard no matter how hard it may be. They know that time is precious and it's either, thin the heard, or die of starvation. It's not greed, it's survival at a whole other level, and it's time to break away to survive.

PILLAR 2: GOALS

Goals are the most important part to any Savages routine, and the third mage pillar of power. This is because without setting goals, a Savage can have no proper heading for their day. Goals are what everybody needs to be setting but aren't. It should be a class of its own in schools, being taught long before adulthood. Dreams without a plan are truly just dreams.

Now, when using Goals, a Savage does it best. They have researched the type of goals they need, the kinds they don't, and they spend time learning the best ways to execute each one flawlessly. Savages know that failing to plan, is planning to fail.

SAVAGE KEY: S.M.A.R.T. Goals

The best news is that each Savage alive today uses, or have used, one single technique to set their goals. No matter who they are, they have used this method for much of their planning and performance monitoring. This method is called S.M.A.R.T. goals.

S.M.A.R.T. isn't just a description for the method employed here. S.M.A.R.T. stands for something…

Specific

Measurable

Attainable

Relevant

Time Based

With this winning formula, Savages have trans-mutated dreams into reality. In sports, they call this much aid "having an edge." Now that we know what that winning edge is, let's look at how it works and exactly what each letter really means for you when you're setting your goals.

Specific means, by definition, clearly defined or identified. How do we clearly identify and define our goals? Simple, we identify exactly what we want when we clearly define what it means to have it. When we know what something means to *us,* we sell ourselves on the idea. How well does this work?

When surveys were conducted on the top-performing sales people on the planet (the Savages), the differentiation, or what made them stand out, from the mediocre to top-dog, was explaining what each feature meant for the customer. This would be enough, but we still have 4 more letters to go over. What will your goals look like when finished?

Measuring goals is the next part of this award-winning (literally) formula. This is the second ingredient to the secret sauce. When the human mind feels that it is winning, it can do incredible things! The affect winning can have on our minds is like taking that game-winning shot where you only hear net.

Setting up check-points that can easily be measured lets a Savage relish in the victories, fueling them for a harder push. It also bolsters their motivation, and sometimes inspires them to do more than they ever even thought possible. Are your goals properly structured to keep you motivated and moving in the right direction?

Attainable goals are the third part of this formula for success and domination. When a Savage sets goals, they make sure they have analyzed it and know that it can actually be achieved. If a goal is not attainable, this can lead to failure. Failure, unlike winning, can kill motivation and wreck one's hope. Once hope is gone, it's all over. NEVER LOSE HOPE!

Now, for a Savage, failure is welcome because without failure, one cannot grow, and a Savage knows this, but a Savage is no fool. Anything a Savage sets his/her mind to can be accomplished, and this to, a Savage KNOWS. Savages set attainable goals. Are your goals attainable?

Relevance is the fourth part to the formula. Setting relevant goals is how Savages stay on the path they have chosen, and ever-moving towards their goals; their definite purpose. Staying relevant is staying focused.

As fierce as a Savage may be, if their goals are not relevant to their dream, it's all for not. Arnold Schwarzenegger once said, "You could have the best ship in the world, but if you don't have a heading, that ship will just drift around never ending up anywhere." I want to hit heavy on the "NEVER" ending up anywhere part. What dreams are your goals related to?

Time Basing is the final part of a legitimate Savages formula for setting goals. When a Savage sets a goal, they always set a time line with it. This holds them accountable for their performance. When they set a time line, it helps them recognize when their performance may be dropping.

Knowing how they are faring with their timeline allows they to notice and reorganize their schedules to readjust their time line or routine to FORCE their goals across the finish line. Are you letting the pace set you up for victory or are you setting the pace of failure?

PILLAR 3: Faith

Faith is the fourth pillar of power and one crucial to any Savages happiness. This is due to the fulfillment a true Savage feels when he/she finally reaches their dream. Faith is what keeps the path straight and the Savage focused.

One of the greatest motivators we will talk about in later chapters is the primary goal of a Savages life; his/her "why." What really separates a Savage from everyone else, is that they have a clear vision and believe they can achieve that vision. Keeping faith is hard. A Savage, however, finds creative ways to keep their faith fresh and always alive. How do they do this? To understand this, we need a prime definition of what faith really is.

SAVAGE KEY: Defining Faith

There are many definitions for faith, but no one has ever been able to define it quit as good as Vusi Thembakwayo. He breaks faith down into 3 different abilities. He says…

"Faith is the ability to

see the invisible,

believe in the impossible,

and trust the unknown."

Now I don't know about you, but this definition really hits the nail on the head. If we can agree that this definition is the best definition, then we are ready to understand what faith really is and means to a Savage. First, we need to break this definition down a little more.

Seeing the invisible is the first part. A Savage knows that to keep his/her faith strong, they need to be able to see their goals completed in their mind long before they actually are. Seeing the invisible means seeing what isn't there… yet.

Believing the impossible is the second part. Savages don't only set goals. Most of the time, what's driving a Savage is a goal so powerful and complex, most people would think it's crazy or way-to-big of a goal. People would call this impossible, but not a true Savage. They believe in the impossible.

Trusting the unknown is the final part. A hardcore Savage knows that this is a needed part of faith. Trusting the unknown means that they put all their cards on the table. They trust that life is working **for them and not to them**. They trust that everything is going to work out for the best even when the odds may be stacked up against them.

Faith isn't a ploy or only a word used in religions around the world. It's a major part of a Savages success and the life choices that result from that success. It's also one the 5 major pillars of power that make a Savage what they are. Faith will make you a true beast and winner, in everything you set your mind to doing or can see accomplished.

PILLAR 4: Focus

Focus pocus. Focus is the fourth major pillar of power and maybe one of a Savages most-useful allies. Many don't know what focus is really is, let alone how to use it to gain a real edge on the battlefield of success and life.

Let's learn what focus really is and how a Savage uses it to better their lives, complete their goals, and thrust ever forward toward their dreams. First, we need to learn what focus really is to a Savage.

SAVAGE KEY: F.O.C.U.S.

Focus has its own many definitions, but the one Savages use is simple and "key." A Savages definition of focus is, **<u>following one course until successful</u>**. To a Savage, focus means following one course of action, one goal, or one mission until it is seen through completely.

A Savage does not let themselves become distracted by other goals or plans until they have successfully completed the one they're working on.

If a Savage has not completed a task, they don't go out with their friends or goof off with buddies. A true Savage sees their goals completed before they reward themselves with enjoyment doing anything else. It's a hard price, but it's a price the Savage is willing to pay.

Another method Savages may use to help keep themselves focus is creating the environment for success. A Savage isn't about to let t.v., friends, or entertainment of any kind distract them from their objective.

To a Savage, creating the environment means setting themselves up for victory by ensuring there is nothing in their environment that can potentially threaten their focus. For example, in a REAL Savages office, there more than likely isn't a television set or video game system. Only permanent equipment used to work.

Savages know that in order to win, they need focus and they will do anything to ensure that focus is uninterrupted.

PILLAR 5: Resolve

Resolve is the last of the 5 mega pillars of power. This is the last major quality of a true Savage. What does a true Savage do when they are chasing their dreams and find out they are failing or stand no chance at reaching it; they keep going. This is the resolve of a Savage, and no one can take that away from them.

David Goggins has a great saying in one of his books, where he talks about taking souls. What he says taking a soul is, is when you let others see you grind so hard that they are lost in disbelief just watching you. You make them feel like there is no stopping, or catching, you. This is what most feel when they see how hard a Savage is willing to grind for the goals they set for themselves. "Dude, he's straight Savage!!!"

Now, how do Savages maintain that resolve? Let's dive a little deeper into the different aspects of Savage resolve and why it makes a Savage who they are.

SAVAGE KEY: Definite Decision

It's not something super complicated that makes a Savages resolve so difficult to understand. A true Savage of success has such a strong resolve because they have made a definite decision about where they want to go and how they want to get there.

Savages ONLY set out after they make this definite decision. This helps them know where they are going and allows them to identify new and evolving paths and which ones to take as they traverse the universe towards their goals.

How does this definite decision allow them to maintain an unrelenting resolve? It all starts with desire, what they want in life or want out of life. Maybe it's something they want to see changed in the world. It all stems from a desire to have something they don't have right now.

Identifying when someone goes savage is normally easy to spot due the success they find now that they have made their definite decision. This decision holds power that most can't understand until they have made their definite decision. What is it that you want to see manifest itself in your life?

Chapter: 2
"How to Unlock Your Savage"

Now that you know what a Savage is, are you a Savage or someone who wants to unlock that potential? If you are a straight up Savage already, congratulations and welcome to the club. If you're not yet a Savage tearing open a path through your goals, it's your lucky day. We are about to break into the reason this book was written, to help you unlock that inner Savage.

Now before you start thinking to yourself "will I have to work hard?" or "will I have to get up early?" The answer is YES! So, if this is the type of commitment that scares you, a commitment to yourself, then I ask that you put down this book and go back to saying "I wish" instead of "I will."

Becoming a Savage is something few ever choose and even fewer ever become. This is because of the incredible sacrifices that you have to make to be a Savage. Which brings me to the first of three main topics we will cover in this chapter; the virtues.

SAVAGE VIRTUE: SACRIFICE

Sacrifice is something NO ONE wants to do because it normally places us outside of our comfort zone. Making a sacrifice literally means to give up something you currently have or could have if chosen. But who wants to do that? Like I said, no one. And that is why Savages are neo-breed beasts of success.

A Savage makes the hardest choices in life simple. They just say no. Does this sound familiar? Maybe you heard your parents say to you before your first sleep over or party. Maybe you had a DARE program back in school that told you "Just say NO!"

Whatever the situation, those who were telling you to just say no couldn't explain WHY it was such a huge deal. They probably couldn't even come up with a reason or example.

Oh, but this time is different isn't it? You know that there is something you want and you know there's something you need to do to get it. But here's the secret; it only takes not doing thongs to get you there. It's really a simple concept; "Just say no."

Not doing a lot of the things you do right now, will give you an extreme amount of time that you don't have right now. *Sacrificing* is never easy, but it doesn't have to be complicated. In fact, it doesn't have to be extreme either. Most things that take your time from you are things you could very easily say "no" to.

When someone asks you to come hangout at the club, watch a movie, or even go for a walk, YOU have the power over your life to say, "I'm sorry, but I'm busy right now." Mel Robbins speaks about this in her book, "The 5 Second Rule." She teaches how the human mind literally talks itself out of making a good decision in as little as 5 seconds.

If we can take this knowledge and apply it to our lives, maybe we can start making the sacrifices we need to make to become Savage beasts who crush every goal they make. Let's not waste the most precious currency we have (Time). Let us resolve to make the right *sacrifices* and save ourselves a life of mediocrity and shameful sheepishly squandered lives.

Now that we know and understand the Savages virtue of *sacrifice*, let's add another

Savage virtue to our minds. Let's start as collection of Savage practices anyone can do and change our lives. This second and more important virtue is a little harder than the last. Let's look into and investigate the Savage virtue of struggle.

SAVAGE VIRTUE: STRUGGLE

What exactly is *struggle* to a Savage? And why is it considered a virtue? Let's open this door and go a little deeper into the realistic behavior of the human mind.

When the average (or even above average) human mind makes sacrifices, they get a shortage of something they are used to getting, probably, a lot of. This can be social time with friends or stimulation from media or videogames. Whatever you sacrifice, will leave a small area of the mind unfulfilled.

Now, can we fill those areas; of course we can. We can even go as far as to say we can put more there then there once was. But how do we do this? The good news is there IS a method we can utilize to upgrade those spaces and it's one Savages use every time they make a sacrifice.

The first part of this method is, you guessed it, *struggle*. The human mind releases one of two types of energy when it is struggling. The first type of energy is obvious. It's the stressful energy that creates tension and lack of focus. Most of the time this energy results in depression. The second type of energy is the raw, beautiful, and Savage creativity.

There's an old quote with some of some sort of importance that said, "There's no such thing as a happy artist." Though I disagree with this statement, it holds a very powerful truth. A person in struggle does have the extreme potential to bring forth the most creative, out-of-the-box art you can find.

Ask any artist and chances are, they will have a dark or hidden secret that eats at them from the deepest parts of their being causing them to struggle. Now maybe they will tell you or maybe they won't. It's entirely up to them. But they are the ones who have learned this incredibly valuable lesson. Silence is sacred.

When we *struggle,* we are doing so because of one of two reasons. Either we have chosen to, or we were forced to. Now, both reasons release energy. Being forced to *struggle* releases that stressful energy while choosing to *struggle* releases that creative energy.

Please note, that both types of energy will carry with them an itch to be filled. However, only one type of energy brings forth that creativity that we desire, that we NEED to push forward and unlock our inner Savage.

Now, just starting to unlock our inner-most Savage, we will probably look at our sacrifices as forced choices we REALLY don't WANT to make. The real question is, how do we change our forced *struggles* into *struggles* by choice?

It starts like this; it's all mental from here. First off, you have more than likely seen the metamorphoses take place right in front of you at some point in your life. It may have been subtle, but I am sure you have seen it somewhere. Here's an example you may have seen.

A spoiled teenager girl is expecting someone to ask them to prom, but instead that special boy asks someone else to prom. That spoiled teenager then says something like, "Pssh, I didn't need him anyway." She continues to tell herself this over and over again.

She may not have even noticed what she did, but if she meant it, she more than likely got a little mad and almost immediately went into using that creative energy to think of some way to get even with someone involved in that situation.

Now, there are certain individuals that can lose something they didn't want to and *immediately* start planning a *creative* way to get revenge or get even. So, what happened there? Did she lose something that she didn't want to lose? I would certainly say so. Should that experience returned to her the energy of stress since she didn't want to lose the chance to go to prom with who she wanted? I would also say yes to this.

So, what did she do to turn that energy around? In almost every case where an individual trans mutates the type of energy they SHOULD receive for the energy they DO receive there's a subtle difference that most have probably never noticed. Those individuals reacted differently than they SHOULD have reacted having just lost something.

Most of the time they get angry or happy instead of sad or oppressed. So, the energy they should receive changes when their reaction changes. This is the secret and I hope you get it. These special cases offer up incredible insight to a simple choice the individuals make. They don't view their sacrifices as lost at all, but gain; a chance to get even or a chance to create. Either way, their circumstances to not affect them on a visual level. They use that energy in another way.

Now that we see what happens to the human mind and the types of energy *struggling* offers up, how do Savages get more of that creativity than anyone else. Why do people call Savages crazy!? Well, my fellow Savages, it's because we are. Our choices are those only a crazy person would make. Why?

SAVAGE VIRTUE: SUFFER

Savages choose to struggle. Once you choose to start struggling, you start to *suffer*. This is because what happens from time to time, shouldn't happen all the time. This is why Savages seem to look so serious or competitive all the time. It changes you and creates a warrior.

But what exactly IS *suffering*? It's a pretty simple concept actually. In the Savage context, *suffering* is when you seem to be in a state of constant grind. This, of course, could not be done if you didn't have the level of creativity and inspiration one can receive from the amount of struggling you do when living at that level.

There is also focus to think about. Losing focus of the main picture can get a lot easier at this level of grind, but if you can remember to stay focused, you can achieve true greatness.

Choosing to live a Savage life isn't always easy, but it has its rewards for sure. *Suffering* is normally something that people definitively try to stay away from. In fact, some of the leading experts in psychology would even say that trying to stay away from *suffering* is the number one root motivator for every choice people make.

What if *suffering* isn't as easy as you thought? Well, you can always find new things to sacrifice that can make the struggles something more doable, but you get out what you put in. And there is only one type of Savage. Those with a truly sick work ethic and unstoppable drive.

Now, *suffering* is only a virtue to the Savage because it must be in order to bring about a new mind; one of creativity and focus. Savages are on the level of making deals with the universe. We know when we pay reciprocity to the universe, it WILL pay us back. So, we gladly offer up what is needed in exchange for what we WILL get in return. It's not easy, but it is always fair.

This is the virtue that most Savages will and do find the hardest. Being able to hold the true Savage level over long periods of time is a hard thing to do. And most can't even fathom how to do this, which I why a true Savage is a rare thing. Even new millionaires will get relaxed when they hit the mark of their first million. Don't be that person.

Which brings me to the next main topic to cover in unlocking your inner Savage. There is a lot of things to take into accountability when choosing to release your inner Savage; Family, friends, work, and even life-style.

So how do Savages work around all of these things? How is living a truly Savage life achievable with a full life? Your about to find out how to use the most influential differentiator in any human's life; waking up.

WAKING UP EARLY

When you *wake up early* you give yourself the best gift you could possibly give. This is because you have just given yourself extra life! For the true Savage, this is an absolute must to unlocking their inner Savage. And if you want to unlock your inner Savage, you're going to have to rise earlier than you do right now as well.

Remember what George Lorimer said, "you have to wake up every morning with determination if you're going to go to bed with satisfaction." Waking up early gives you the time you NEED without interruptions or distractions. It's the purest time of the day.

Even Hal Elrod, author of The Miricle Morning speaks about how focused, productive, and successful mornings generate focused, productive, and successful days. He goes on to state that this inevitably does lead to a successful life.

If you're looking to unlock that true inner Savage, you're going to have to wake up early. There is simply no replacement for it. Extraordinary success truly comes from waking up early. Have you ever heard it said that if you want a better life, you have to make better choices?

I truly know this to be fact, but there is another quote that also says if you want something you've never had, you have to do things you've never done. I hold more to this one only because I believe it helps me remember not to live the same day twice. Life is too short to live the same day.

If you truly want that Savage life, this is the game changer that will get you there. But how can you find the motivation or passion to wake up early every morning? E.T. (the hip-hop preacher) says his dreams wake him up every morning.

There is a secret to success and unlocking your inner Savage hidden in what he says here. Which brings me to my third and last main topic to spit on and probably the most important one; Savage Growth.

SAVAGE GROWTH

Savage growth is very important. Savage growth is what sets the curve at which a Savage grows into what they will become. Savages have also learned the best way to accomplish this as well. The secret to exceptional and savage growth is this; consistent improvement. The key to consistently improving is a very delicate formula that has remained secret until now.

Our minds are very complicated, but it turns out, humans are getting smarter and have learned how we, well, learn. I am about to give you the secret to Savage growth and how to maintain consistent improvement. This is the full proof way I have learned to keep the consistency, not just sustained but, in FULL effect. On piece of paper or in your notebook, write these words on separate lines.

- Read
- Hear

- Watch
- Discuss
- Teach

Each one of these words is one method way we learn. Humans have learned that we retain and hold onto 10% of what we read, 20% of what we hear, 50% of what we watch (video w/sound), 70% of what we discuss, and a massive 95% of what we teach. The secret to keeping your domination in motion is to, not use only one but, use all of these methods each and EVERY day.

This may sound pretty easy, but it is not as easy as you may think. Let's think about this for just a second. You have to find time to read, listen, watch, discuss, AND teach someone every single day to maximize your power.

It may sound hard and you be thinking to yourself, "man, I hardly have time to myself as it is every day." Now, I don't know about you, but if my performance depended on the amount of power I have and can direct towards my project, I'm going to want my power source to be a massive force capable of withstanding untold amounts of strain. I wouldn't want it to be invincible so nothing could stop it.

So, how do we carve out the time? Where do we find the energy and the focus? Fear not, I am about to give you the single most powerful method and just about the only way you can pull off becoming a true savage that nothing can hold and no one can stop. Are you ready?... Here it is. WAKE UP!!!

There is one thing every savage has had in common. One thing that made them true savages of nature. Those with disgusting work ethics and a truly nasty grind every single day. It was their morning.

I once heard, "the morning breeze holds the secrets to success." I have found this to be of true value in my life. When I first started to rise in the morning, I found purpose. And there is no catalyst like purpose. Your purpose is your why; the reason you wake up each morning. Your why is your destiny, pure and simple.

All you need to do to obtain this is *know your future.* I won't go into that right now, that is truly a high-level savage lesson, but don't worry, we will definitely cover it in the next chapter. Just know that it's extremely important to have a "why" to maintain focus as you move forward in the journey of a true savage. Right now, we will stick with waking up. It's hard, I know, but also necessary.

Waking up while most of your friends and family are still sleeping ensures, at the least, 2 things. The first is, people are going to think you are truly insane. And the earlier you get up, the more insane they will think you are, but let them. While life is happening TO them, it's going to be happening FOR you. The second thing waking up ensures you is peace and quiet.

Peace and quiet early in the morning is one of a true Savages greatest weapons. Why? Because only during this time can a real Savage really grind without the common sheep (people who aren't Savages) getting in your way.

Chapter: 3
"The Savage Handbook"

Before we break into the different strategies you can use to ensure your Savage victories, the tools and tips that will add height to your game and have you slamming on the challenges ahead, let me first say congratulations. You are making the best decision of your life.

Living the life of a true Savage is not easy, and let me say to all those already-Savages reading this, without you, the world would not have the hope it has now. You know who you are and now it's time to rise and do more than we have ever done to ensure a better world and a better us.

Without further a due, let's dive into the collection of tools, tips, and strategies I have taken and used from the greatest mentors, masters, and experts and have put to the test. These are just a few of the tools, tips, and strategies I have proven work.

Let's give you some weapons to win you upcoming Savage battles. Let's help you unleash that inner Savage. As you read on, you will learn which areas are some of the most important areas to safe-guard and build onto to improve really walk it like you talk it as you unlock your true potential. Take these tips, tools, and strategies and weave them into your life and become the Savage you were really meant to be.

YOUR DAILY SCHEDULE

Your daily schedule is your road map for the day. It's kind of like your compass. It keeps you on a track and living days of your own design. Setting a daily schedule is incredibly important to a Savage.

Scheduling helps you keep track of your time. Time is the most valuable currency you have. Every single minute is a coin you can never get back and how you spend these coins will show. Are you investing them the right way or are you squandering them by wasting time?

Set a schedule and win like the pros. Know where your time is going and how it's being used. This is how Savages know their doing the right thing and investing their time correctly.

YOUR MORNING ROUTINE

Creating a great morning routine is vital to owning your day. When you crush your morning, you crush your day. There is no substitute for a good morning routine.

Your morning routine sets the pace for the entire day. Getting a lot done in the early morning hours helps you maintain a winner's energy and mentality throughout your whole day. The morning is when the true Savage shines. Children think it's cool to stay up late. A Savage knows waking up early is real boss stuff.

Start your day off right. Give yourself the gift of a winner's mentality. Never substitute your morning routine for anyone or anything. Keep your morning YOUR morning. Master your morning and master life.

YOUR MENTORS

It's true that who you hang around lets you know who you are, but what about who you look up to? To model the best, you have to learn from the best. There are so many good role models and HIGHLY successful Savages in the world. These are the individuals you need to study. Learn what they do and then model that behavior and/or habits.

Mentors help direct you. They steer you in the right direction and help you make the right choices. Mentors are where Savages turn to for wisdom and insight. A real Savage will always keep their stock of mentors fresh and ever-growing.

Make the right choice and follow the right people. Find yourself some mentors and copy them. Do what they do and watch yourself become more than you are right now. Who will you choose?

YOUR EDUCATION

It has been said that education is the great equalizer. This is so true. Education doesn't always have to cost money. There are so many ways to be educated or even to self-educate. We just mentioned mentors. They can teach you, but you can also learn from libraries, the internet, and a plethora of other places and sources.

Education can give you the edge you need to outperform your old self. It improves you. It can also help you meet your goals and set higher dreams for yourself. The sky is the limit where education is concerned. You can learn anything and the real Savage will use this to their advantage.

Do you think it's time for an upgrade? Isn't it time to start the real growth? Education is how it's done. What will you learn? How will you improve yourself?

YOUR DIET

It's true that your performance is based on your fuel and the human body is no different. You are what you eat. If you want to perform above average, you need to eat above average. If you are truly modeling the greatest Savages on Earth, your diet will change.

A better diet raises your performance on a visual level, but the real performance change happens on the inside. When you invest in a better diet, your mind will work faster, more focused, and consistently improve your creativity. Don't lose your edge to other Savages because you don't want to have the discipline to add better foods to your diet.

You don't have the time to waste. You're already late to the game. Do you really have the time not to use every advantage in your tool bag?

Will you become the winner that creates his/her performance through their diet?

YOUR FRIENDS

Who you choose to have around you, lets you know who you are. You don't want to fill your personal environment with people who aren't going to push you to keep momentum, to keep pushing forward, and to keep winning like a Savage.

When you start to better yourself, you have to thin the herd. Sorting the company you keep will impact your mood and the level of motivation you feel more often and the quality of life you live. Thin your herd.

Better friends are a sign of maturity. Maturity leads to real-boss-stuff. This is due in part to the amount you're able to get done because of the time you save not entertaining dumb ideas or activities. But another part is that so will your better friends. This can be a huge help in the war on distraction.

YOUR CAR

Now, I know what you're thinking, "He's gonna talk about getting the nicest car so I can look like a real Savage." However, the truth couldn't be anymore opposite. Buying a really nice car can set you back a lot. This can weigh you down on your road to success.

When buying a car, you need to think functionality over aesthetics (looks). It's a very true statement to say that the poor stay poor trying to look rich while the rich stay rich acting like they're poor. I could stay on this topic a while, but to keep it brief, a big deciding factor in finance is how well your purchasing discipline is towards necessity over desire.

So, save your money like a rich man. Brian Tracy says, "Live like no one else will so you can live like no one else will." He is very right on this. Save and invest. Live like a pro and perform like a true Savage. Don't buy a brand-new car.

YOUR JOURNAL

If you are headed for success and you know it, you're going to want to keep a journal. For me, it's a collection on small pocket-sized notebooks. These have helped me keep schedules, align my goals, and stay focused. However, keeping a journal will also help you remember your journey, which can be just as valuable in you later years.

When you keep a journal on you at all times, you're telling the world you are ready for the next lesson. You're saying, "I'm always prepared to learn the next new thing." This can help you bring up great ideas or remember lessons you may otherwise forget.

Will you take the pledge to keep record of you travels through your transformation? Will you be ready the next time the universe has some wisdom to impart to you? Take this to heart. Not everyone does this, but it is definitely something a true Savage does. Keep your journal on you.

YOUR EXERCISE

Staying healthy is key, sure, but when you exercise, more happens than you know. Working out in the morning can raise your bodies reactions and thought time for the rest of the day. It also releases endorphins in the mind that give you the winners mentality. Riding this energy can help you achieve outstanding results throughout your day!

When you make time to exercise each and every day, you keep your mind and body in sync and maintain a habit that can save your life. Many of the world's richest wish, above anything else, for more time. Health is very important. Your goals and dreams depend greatly on your health.

Discipline your mind now to force your body to change. This will be your greatest gift to yourself. Every true Savage trains their mind and their body. Do what is needed, make the hard choices my brothers and sisters and ascend all the way into greatness.

YOUR CELEBRATIONS

The way you celebrate says a lot about who you are and what's important to you. Most people blow huge amounts of money on useless things like drinks or drugs. Don't be those guys. Real Savages reach for a higher level of celebration that involves only their small circle of friends. They normally have great food they prepare themselves and light drinks as they talk over the next step in their plan.

When we celebrate it also engages a strong energy of success and victory. NOT passing the opportunity up to celebrate is extremely important, but only if you're celebrating right. Allowing time to stop and live in the moment gives you a huge advantage that most don't know about.

The feeling of victory naturally doesn't last long and fades away soon. This comes because most are looking for happiness and no number of victories will give them this. So, they usually waste this possible momentum and bypass celebrations all together. But when a Savage has claimed victory, they celebrate smart and enjoy bettering themselves while engaging in that energy and riding the momentum forward.

Chapter: 4
"Savage Companionship"

I want to take a chapter out and hit on a topic most people don't know about. It's just another aspect of a strong Savage pursuing their dreams; however, it can hold immense value for you along your journey. It is also true that obtaining this gift is hard, but even harder to maintain.

The hardest battles in life are those that take place inside your own head. These words have been told for a very long time and they are just as true today as the first time they were spoken. In a Savages life, those battles are no different. Knowing this, you should want the most help you can get to combat these battles.

I'm about to tell you one way you can, not just bolster your defenses in these battles of the mind, but also strengthen your offense so you can win the war. What we are going to cover in this chapter is Savage companionship (the realest relationship(s) you will ever have) and the benefits they can offer a Savage tearing up the field of success.

In this chapter we are going to talk about *3 different types of companionship* a Savage couldn't be luckier to have in their corner and the reason *most Savages won't have them.* We are also going to go over the a few of the *deceptive types of companionship* that can be TOXIC and a huge stumbling block on your road to success, but also in your life.

First, let's examine the positive types of companionship that Savage should always be on the lookout for and strive to keep in their corner. The first type of companionship we will cover is the brotherhood.

BROTHERHOOD

It's an extremely small contribution to say that having a brother or sister in your corner for the battles you will face along your journey is the most empowering attribute you can possess. A brother (or sister) can offer a plethora of precious wisdom, fresh perspectives, and direction. They can create inspiration when your lost, build motivation when your, and bestow hope in dark times.

I have been so fortunate to possess this type of companionship in my life and it has been an irreplaceable crutch after the battles of life have taken their toll. But brothers are so much more. This type of companionship offers aid because even if your goals are different, the drive is the same and this means you can reinforce progress in each other's lives and watch the victories tally up.

Having a brother in battle can also mean not being blind-sided when the enemies that will try to ride your success into the ground. It also means when you have been wounded by life or something along the journey, you have someone there that you can count on; someone who can drag you to safety and help mend your injuries. Brothers are truly the strongest force for success you can have by your side.

It's so rare to find someone who is going the same direction as you and who understands the transformation you are going through as you unlock your inner savage. However, it's far rarer to be able to accompany someone undergoing that same transformation. This is one reason finding the brotherhood companionship can be so hard, but once you find it, do all you can to keep him/her in your corner. There is no replacement for that kind of relationship.

Finally, there's reciprocity. Reciprocity is the price you're willing to pay now for what you're going to get. It's kind of like reaping what you so or karma. What goes around comes around? There are many words for it, but what a brother offers is also the opportunity to help someone in ways no one else can help that person. No one can really understand a person trying to unlock, or even live, their inner Savage accept another person attempting the same feat or achievement.

Knowing exactly what a fellow brother (or sister) is going through could offer the opportunity to better their lives or journey in a real way. However, there is also the flip side of this arrangement. If you are placed in the position to help someone attempting the incredible feat of unlocking their inner Savage and do nothing when aid is needed, God, life, or the universe will also see and reciprocity will once again take its sweet justice and you will feel reciprocity on a physical, financial, or mental level.

I guess the old man was right; with great power comes great responsibility. So, do yourself a favor or two. If you find the companionship a brother or sister can offer, do not let it go. And if you are ever placed in the position to do extreme good, DO IT. And watch God, life, or the universe reward you in phenomenal ways.

MENTORSHIP

Mentors hold a unique power and ability to navigate the minefields of success, the trenches of achievement, and the frontlines of prosperity. Mentors appear to hold the keys to advancement and know when you're ready to use them. As mentors, we have had the experience to walk through many fires and have vowed to continue to walking through them in order to help as many as we can.

As a mentor myself, I have had the unique pleasure of help more people than I can count and will continue to help anyone I am in a position to better or direct down a more prosperous path to greatness. However, mentors are not all-knowing or beyond failure ourselves. We will stumble and fall from time to time, as I have in past times. What makes a mentor different from others is that we will NEVER give up. If we do not give up, we cannot fail.

Finding a mentor can be one of the greatest experiences of your life. Mentors can offer tremendous value to your life, if you're willing to accept it. If you ever find the companionship of a mentor, do not waste it because just as you are progressing, they are as well and may not be around long. So, always seek to accept their teachings and use their knowledge to thrust forward on the path to success and greatness. Another great trait of mentors is that they love what they do and will always offer help where and when they can.

Now, mentors are incredible aids and probably best used for the wealth of experience they can bring to that metaphorical table we mentioned before. However, stumbling across mentor who has fully released their inner Savage may be a lot easier to identify. We see them all the time and hear them everywhere. Les Brown, Tony Robbins, E.T. (the hip hop preacher),

Dwane 'the Rock' Johnson, and many more you have come to know by name are all mentors who have unlocked that inner Savage game upon the world.

These mentors can add the same kind of wealth and value to your life, but they do it on a far greater scale. They have come to realize what you will soon realize as well; that your time is precious and more valuable than any other currency you own. But they too realize that reciprocity is real and because they are in positions to do the most help, they must do a lot more. I once heard it put in a way that struct me to the bone. It was a quote that said, "Put the universe in your debt with how much good you do."

Again, we see how reciprocity is both respected and feared even among the strongest Savages on Earth. What Savage mentors are most used for, for to those who can get a hold of them, are more to their particular specialties. To the broader base of those who watch in aww at the majestic flight of the true Savages of the world is affirmations and positive reinforcement when and where you need it through your television, pc, phone, magazine, or book. They can literally be found just about everywhere, ready to share the gospel of success and pure Savage results of hard work with any and all who are willing to listen.

If you are blessed to have a mentor bestowed upon you, count yourself as highly favored by the universe to have had the fortune of possessing the companionship of a mentor.

MARRIAGE

The last type of companionship you will most definitely want to have in your corner is that of a spouse, but not any husband or wife can cut it with someone who has truly unlocked their inner Savage. Once the Savage is released, there is no safe way to put it back. They will not stop; they will not give up. For this reason, they need someone who falls into a VERY strict variety; a true class of their own.

The incredible gift of a wife (or husband) that stays by your side through it all is irreplaceable. However, finding a spouse that will remain by your side through the worst times and still hold their head up at your side, a spouse that will push you even when you have stopped pushing yourself, a spouse that won't let you give up or give in. These are the only spouses capable of withstanding the extreme adversity and unbreakable resolve given to a man or woman who has truly released their inner Savage.

These spouses know when it's time to step up and do their part, but also how to spend countless hours, days, or even months away from their Savage so that the Savage can do what it must to shred through life and massacre all tests that say they aren't ready to advance in their field. A true Savage knows the worth of these spouses and will fight to maintain a healthy relationship with them.

In this type of companionship, there is no room for weakness and error. If mistakes are made, they work through them. If problems arise, they both do what is needed to arrange a solution. There is never a circumstance that cannot be remedied or corrected. This is where relationships of a human kind top out. Up here, an understanding of sacrifices is held in the mind of both the Savage and the spouse. And both know that nothing mental, physical, or monetary is beyond the reckoning of the war. The war of the inner Savage.

THE OTHER SIDE

Next, we are going to examine 3 deceptive types of companionship that can poison even the hardest efforts a Savage puts forth. These sorts of companionships are the most dangerous to success and true victory over your dreams. Have no fear though, there are ways to identify these types of companionships and how to rid yourself of each one. Let's dive in and learn how.

The first thing to know is that, once the inner Savage has been released, ridding yourself of a bad companionship is like swatting an insect. But make no mistake, these insects are each unique and offer different challenges to overcome. Swatting these insects may take more than a motion of hand.

For this explanation, we will use three different insects most have heard of (but you can 'google' any you don't know); the fly, the leech, and the prey mantis. You will see how each are unique in the abilities and talents, but each also has it's on unique identifiers that make them easy to identify. Remember, identifying is only the first step of ridding yourself of a bad companion.

THE FLY

The party animal.

The *fly* is a fun type of friend. They find every reason in the book to go out and party every night. *Flys* love to take you "under their wing" and desire to help you through your problems. This often involves drinking away your feelings or traveling other avenues to forget your circumstances rather than facing them. For this reason, *flies* appear to be the good kind of person to keep around. This is dangerous to someone who's trying to unlock their true inner Savage.

As your life improves, your life will get harder. Unlocking the inner Savage and releasing it upon the world is a route many don't or can't follow. There will always be problems to face and if your drink or party them away, you will NEVER step up and move past that barrier that separates the Savage from the common man.

Now, *flies* will often possess a good heart or nature which also makes them appear to be selfless, but inside they are not. *Flies* desire a companion above all else. They want more than anything to have a brother or sister who is always ready to party with them and escape the true realities of life. It may not always be obvious because the attitude of a *fly* is always upbeat and happy, but they are almost always suffering in their careers, with their families, or financially.

Now, what makes *flies* such a deceptive companionship is that they can identify god decisions and will even make an effort to better themselves, at least for a short while. Due to their basic instincts however, they will always return to their instinctual escape from responsibility and commitment. And if you are with them, they will also do whatever they can to drag you back with them. After all, *flies* are your friends (and often times, your best friend).

It's not always easy to thin the herd and cut the bad from your life, but it's even harder when you can't see that it's bad. This is why *flies* are so dangerous to the journey. They want to change, but can't, or won't. They are, and will always, be stuck. *Flies* will never ascend like you will. Stay away from them and pursue the highest goals for yourself. As you climb ever higher and higher, they will lose grip of you. They won't be able to hold on as you speed towards success. They will eventually fall back to the ground and you will shed them from your life.

From this point, you only need to make the effort to not fall back into another deceptive companionship with another *fly*. Unfortunelty, there will always be more *flies*, always buzzing around, always getting in your way, and always trying to distract you and steal your focus. Don't let them. Break away and steer clear of these companionships.

Have you ever been walking past some trash pile and the *flies* come buzzing around? What do you do to keep them from buzzing all around you? Normally you start walking faster to escape them. The same is with this deceptive companionship. The faster you race towards success, the harder it will be for *flies* to buzz around and steal your focus away from what really matters.

THE LEECH

The user.

The *leech* is the type of person who preys on good hearts and generosity. They appear broken and unable, but they are smart and incredible at swindling. This is how they live. The truth is, they found it easier to live as a victim than victor. They enjoy playing the "why me?" games with anyone willing to listen.

The *leech* doesn't really have a career, but hops job to meaningless job over the course of their life to escape comfortability. They will never find the real happiness they desire deeply within, because they are too busy seeking comfort in the now. They will often use you for your generosity among other things. They will make all your contributions seem small or your sacrifices insignificant.

The *leech* often puts others down or finds reasons to crack jokes about others in an effort to lighten the feeling of lack of real commitment in their own lives. This makes them less than desirable to be around, so the quality of their friends are often like-minded individuals with no real purpose or goals. Most of the time, *leeches* will have other *leeches* as friends or company.

Now, the reason *leeches* are so deceptive is because they are hood at identifying and exploiting the weaknesses of those they use. Though most of the time they use your heart against you, they may also use an addiction, a crush, relative, or even your own friends against you.

Have you ever crossed a deep creek or went swimming in a pond only to find that you are now covered in *leeches*? Well, these metaphorical *leeches* are exactly the same. Whenever possible, *leeches* will try to work with other *leeches*. They will try to beat you down emotionally in an effort to exacerbate you for your money, assets, or value. Ever heard, "Well you gave him some! I want some too!?" This really happens more often than you think, especially in a world full of different, and often entitled, individuals who don't want to work for anything!

The main reason *leeches* are so dangerous to the journey is because, people ALL have a sense of good. We know right from wrong, but only the lowest will capitalize on it. *Leeches* do just that. Capitalize on your good. With bugs like these, who needs enemies.

Squash them and get them out of your life as soon as possible. More often than not, the only way to do this is to put your foot down and give them an ultimatum (options they can't refuse). Don't continue to let them use you! You're better than that and they will hold you down to their level, happily siphoning off all you own or can offer.

If you have a *leech* problem, let them know today that it's over, you refuse to be subjected to this one-sided relationship any longer. As a last-ditch effort, they may make one final attempt at keeping you. This is normally a gift or small attempt to return your favors. That is not what you are looking for. You want freedom from the *leech*. It's time to pull them off and let them suck on another.

THE PREY MANTIS

The influencer.

The *prey mantis* is a stealthy and cunning person. It lays hidden watching and waiting for the perfect moment to snap. This type of companionship will often last the longest and is the hardest to dissolve. I felt it needed to be included due to the damage it always and inevitably leaves behind.

While the *prey mantis* may be a largely involved in your life, they want nothing more than to mis-lead you and manipulate you. They want to see you damage yourself and watch you fall. These types of companions are the absolute worst to be involved with. You never see them coming before it's way too late.

One way a *prey mantis* will give themselves away is by making a move. Just like a literal *prey mantis*, the metaphorical *prey mantis* will also only drop its camouflage when they make a move. They will often influence from behind the seen, but sometimes, they come out in the open and work against you by openly volunteering you for something you try to turn down.

Sometimes the *prey mantis* will influence you during social situations in an attempt to embarrass yourself or try something dangerous. Remember, they don't care about your well-being. They only want to see you damage yourself. On the more damaging occasions, they may sway you from making the best decisions of your life.

When someone really good comes into your life, they may try to separate you from them by using your own feelings against you. They make you feel bad for wanting something better than you have now. This is an outrage! Someone trying to unlock their inner Savage NEEDS to better themselves. Unfortunelty, the *prey mantis* will always be on the lookout for ways to make you fail or fall hard. This is why you must always be on the lookout as well.

Always observe what people are telling you. Your closest family and friends will often be the first to tell you that you can't do something or shouldn't do this or that. This doesn't always mean they are against you deliberately, but the *prey mantis* likes to stay close to its prey. Besides, success is impossible without failure. Failure is the best teacher!

The *prey* mantis likes to stay close to its prey. They are normally always someone close to you. If you think that you may be in this deceptive companionship, try to test those around you. Offer a problem you already know the answer to. Sometimes they just can't help themselves; they have to see what will happen, so they will give you worst advice even if it means giving themselves away.

Sometimes the signs are subtle, but sometimes they are obvious as well. Look out for those who brag about the dumb stuff you're willing to do to everyone. They often-times want to see if others have a more creative mind than they do and will offer new way to destroy yourself.

To release yourself from the talons of the *prey mantis* you are going to have to search yourself deep and find strength you may not even know lies within you. Never doubt yourself. Never give up. Seek help if you need to. If help is the route you want to take, once you give them the situation, listen and observe, but do not take real advice for granted. If they are looking out for you in a real way, they will do what is necessary to help you. Do not stop them or let your deceived heart get in the way of your progress.

While the *prey mantis* may be near impossible to identify or even spot sometimes, they aren't invincible and can be dealt with, but these types of companionships cannot be allowed to go on if you are going to release your inner Savage. Break away and be free from the lies. Don't be eaten alive by the *prey mantis*.

Chapter: 5
"Your Savage Purpose"

<u>YOUR SAVAGE PURPOSE</u>

It's been called many things, from "your why" to "your definite purpose." It is the one deciding factor that will give you that even bigger boost of focus, creativity, and drive you need to find yourself living your dreams and completing your goals like a true Savage of success.

Your purpose is what you want to accomplish in your life. It's what you can see yourself with at the end of all your hard work. *Your Savage purpose* is what lies beyond that. *Your Savage purpose* is what calls you. It's what you were born to do, who you were born to be, why you were born.

It has been said that true fulfillment can only come from seeking that which is above you. A true Savage has realized this and will attempt to transcend who, what, and where they are now to accomplish this. Real Savages will sacrifice everything to achieve this higher transcendence. Often times, the true Savages' philosophy is more than most will ever be able to handle. Purpose; how does one describe it?

I once heard it described by a stranger's poetry like this, "To accept your fate with pleasure, knowing that you have finally completed what your creator intended for you." It's nearly impossible for a Savage to describe what calls them forward, but they hear it as clear as the air that envelopes all of us.

Your Savage purpose may not always be told, but it can always be heard.

I want to share with you what it is, who has it, and what it could mean for you. We all engage different paths, but the truest paths are our own. I want to open your eyes to something you've never heard before; something you do not know. Humans were created with one unique ability that only we possess. This is the ability to transform into a completely different being; a being of complete variation.

We see this happen in Christianity when someone is "born again." We see this happen sometimes when someone undergoes a traumatic experience that leaves them changed and different. These individuals are forever changed and incapable of ever returning to the state they were once in. Finally, we see it in the Savage.

When a someone truly wishes with all their heart and soul to become something different, something more, the universe answers the call. And as the Savage begins their journey towards the call, the change and the things they were once, they are not any more. Should it ever come that the Savage has lost their way, they may fall, but the call is still there. The purpose is still there... waiting.

THE THREE QUESTIONS

What is my Purpose?

How do I find it?

Can I reach it?

The answers to these questions are of extreme value. Each of these questions are particular to you as they are to me and each answer will be different and for each person. You may ask "is that even possible?!" and I would simply say "yes." Partly because it's meaning is so difficult to understand, but also because there are so few real Savages in the world when compared to the human population.

  To tell you what your purpose is would be to lie, because only the universe and you know that. It is only possible for you to know it for only you can hear the call. No one's purpose is the same and no two people can hear the same call. In the end, one will concede to the other knowing that the calling they have heard, was not theirs, but someone else's and they may only be meant to help aid that individual on their journey to see a calling fulfilled. Either way, both have fulfilled their individual purposes.

  Finding your purpose, however, is easier than you might expect; for it actually finds you. They say that when you are ready, the master will appear. This is true. As long as you push yourself to get better, the right one will come along and you will learn your purpose. The hardest part of this stage is just getting to the point where you are ready and consistently stay that way. Life will always show mercy, we need only be ready when that mercy is shown and we will find our purpose; or rather, it will find us.

Reaching your purpose is not always hard, but it's not always easy either. It all depends on the calling you hear. What I can tell you is that it is possible and you need only know that it is to achieve it. I have always said that belief is a weak word watered down over generations to mean something "could be true." When we KNOW something, however, it is fact in our minds and we can see it as if it is real. We know it will come to pass, because it is without question.

HOW PURPOSE SEPERATES

Any Savage can tell you that, just like any other human on Earth, they would lose focus and direction if it were not for their purpose. I recently met an individual who claims it's called being a wondering essential. He explained to me that it's having the motivation and drive to work hard and keep yourself ready, but with no definite goal in mind.

The wondering essentialist is someone who doesn't know their purpose yet, but they maintain the essentials needed to start moving towards a Savage purpose. Without a Savage purpose you are only a wondering essentialist. An individual improving his ship, but having no heading. This is how purpose separates.

A Savage has so much momentum that they cannot be stopped. Having a purpose allows this momentum to build up more than someone without a defined and focused path. When you have no definite purpose, you can move, sure, but eventually you must slow down again once whatever you're working on has been mastered or completed.

When you're a real Savage, you have something that may take a long time to reach and even longer to master. This means that you have the rest of your life to build up momentum and traverse a focused path that will keep us moving forward; not in every direction short-term goals (and even some long-term goals) lead us.

IDENTIFYING YOUR PURPOSE

Identifying you purpose could be a hard thing to do, so here I would like to give you a few tips and clues to look for when you are ready to find your purpose. And just know that if your purpose changes, that's alright. Change directions and start moving in the direction of your new purpose, but only you know, and only you can make that choice.

The first clue to knowing you have found your Savage purpose is when you have planned and resolved to accomplish something almost no one thinks you can accomplish. People may encourage you, but here their encouragement can't reach. They may think to themselves, "well I only meant do better" or "I didn't mean all that!"

Even the most encouraging friends and/or family will set beliefs for how far they think you can go. People without the Savage mind have a bad habit of doing that. A you will need to look elsewhere for the encouragement you need to stay on the path. You will need to find true encouragement with no limits. Belief that won't end with a pre-set limit.

The next clue normally comes following the first. One sure fire way you can tell you have found your Savage purpose is because you will face opposition from those you trust and look to the most for motivation and belief in you. When your friends and family tell you that you can't do this or that, you are almost sure to have found your Savage purpose.

It's not because they have changed, they only want what's best for you, but according to the average mind, not the Savage mind. They are only trying to protect you, but only from something they can't see. If you can see it, and see it clearly, then move in that direction and never give up. Which brings me to my next clue.

When you have found your Savage purpose, you won't quit trying to achieve or build it even when all seems to have gone wrong and everything comes crashing down around you. If your purpose can keep you getting up over and over again, failure after failure, then you may have found your true Savage purpose.

A Savage purpose will never let you give up or quit trying. It will not let you give up. Savage purpose has an itch that won't let you quit until you see it completed your way. It's almost like you know you will die if you don't see it completed. You now, know your Savage purpose. Just remember, this may change, but it's not likely to.

The next clue you may find that will almost surely tell you that you have found your Savage purpose is that it's something you can't do right now. It's normally something you can't do even after a long time. Your Savage purpose is normally something that will take a lifetime to build or create.

Don't worry too much about the process though, a true Savage will love the process. They love the grind. You will to. When you love learning and building what you need to reach your Savage purpose, you will find it easy to do.

The next clue is when you realize you haven't been using you alarm clock anymore and still get up extremely early. When you wake up wanting to better yourself or build your mind, this is when you know you are moving in the right direction.

Savage purpose has a way of whispering in your ear, that it's time to wake up. It can't let you sleep long before you need to start moving again. When your mind has found the focus it needs, the dream of a true Savage, it automatically knows how fast you need to move in order to accomplish that dream in order to reach it before death.

The last clue, but certainly not the least, is when your dream will change the world over. When what you're working on will make the world change its views or the way it operates, you know you have found your Savage purpose. This is because a Savage can't leave the world the same way it was when he entered it. The call inside will not let him or her.

Do you know your purpose will change the world? Do you think it can change the way the world operates? Can you reach it the way you are now, or do you need to become the type of person who can reach that dream?

FINAL WORDS

We have covered a lot in a short amount of time. Sometimes a book can be the start of a journey, or the end of one. For me, this book is the start. I hope you enjoyed it and are ready for more, because I don't plan on stopping and can't wait to see how my writing impacts all who will read it.

Until next time, I hope you Release Your Savage...

-Rico Piddington

www.ingramcontent.com/pod-product-compliance
Lightning Source LLC
Chambersburg PA
CBHW030454220526
45464CB00006B/2534